CLASSIC MARQU

# Trams of the British Isles
## 1945-1962

PETER WALLER

NOSTALGIA ROAD

First published by
Crécy Publishing Limited 2013

A CIP record for this book is available from
the British Library

**ISBN 9781908 347213**

Printed in Malta by Melita Press

**Nostalgia Road is an imprint of**
**Crécy Publishing Limited**
1a Ringway Trading Estate
Shadowmoss Road
Manchester M22 5LH

**www.crecy.co.uk**

*Front Cover:* Built in two batches by Brush (Nos 255-63) and English Electric (Nos 264-71), the 17 cars that became known as 'Middleton Bogies' were fitted with Maley & Taunton swing link bogies and were delivered to Leeds between 1933 and 1935. The last of the type were to survive in service until 1957. *Ray Bicknese/Online Transport Archive*

*Rear Cover Top:* During the 1930s, Liverpool under the management of W G Marks was at the forefront of tramway modernisation in Britain, with new routes, many built of private reservations, and new trams, such as the 'Baby Grands' (illustrated here). In the late 1940s, however, a switch of policy saw the tramways quickly abandoned, with the last trams operating in 1957. *John B McCann/Online Transport Archive*

*Rear Cover Bottom:* Blackburn No 58 was one of a batch of 40 bogie cars built by G F Milnes; originally open-top, all but eight were rebuilt as fully enclosed by 1935. *F N T Lloyd-Jones/Online Transport Archive*

*Contents Page:* London Transport No 1923, an 'E/3' class car dating from 1931, pictured at Abbey Wood with a service towards the Embankment. The 38 was one of the London routes to survive until the final closure in July 1952. *Harry Luff/Online Transport Archive*

# CONTENTS

# Introduction

In 1939 for the second time in less than a generation, Britain and its Empire found itself involved in a World War. Unlike World War 1, which had been fought largely in the trenches of northern France and in the various theatres of operation overseas, World War 2 was to have a dramatic impact on the lives of those at home, with the threat posed by the German air force initially and later from the flying bombs. Most significant towns and cities suffered some damage during the war as the Germans sought to destroy British industry, transport and morale.

In the years leading up to the outbreak of war in September 1939 there had been a considerable decline in the number of tramway operators in the British Isles, but there still remained some 50 operators of varying sizes. There were four in Scotland — Aberdeen, Dundee, Edinburgh and Glasgow — or five if the freight-only line at Cruden Bay is included; four in Wales — Cardiff, Llandudno & Colwyn Bay, Great Orme and Swansea & Mumbles — as well as six on the island of Ireland — Belfast, Bessbrook & Newry, Dublin, Fintona, Giant's Causeway and Hill of Howth — and a number in England, from Bristol in the southwest to Newcastle and Sunderland in the northeast and from Blackburn and Bury in Lancashire to London and Southampton in the south. Even with the pre-war abandonments, most significant towns and cities in England, with the exception of places like Nottingham and Derby, still possessed some tramcar routes. Many of these systems, however, like Bradford, London and Manchester, had been converting their routes to either bus or trolleybus operation during the 1930s and so many of the surviving systems were a fraction of the size that they had been at their peak.

With Britain at war, all the country's efforts had to be turned to the fight; there was, therefore, little scope for major innovations in terms of public transport and this included effectively a moratorium on tramway conversions. In London, the early months of the war saw the final tram to trolleybus conversions in the capital, but these were atypical. Elsewhere the 'make do and mend' mentality meant that the tram battled on; indeed, there were odd services — such as that serving Undercliffe in Bradford — that were restored where surviving infrastructure permitted.

Britain's trams were, however, not to be immune from the damage wrought by the Luftwaffe during the war and two systems — Bristol and Coventry — were both to be finally closed as a result of enemy action. Both systems had been contracting prior to the outbreak of war but had been reprieved once hostilities broke out; the massive damage that Coventry suffered in November 1940 was to lead to the final abandonment there. Elsewhere, the tramways of London suffered significant

The largest system to survive World War 2 was that serving Glasgow with a fleet in excess of 1,000 trams. The largest element of the fleet were the 'Standard' cars built between 1898 and 1924 such No 48 seen here at Millerston on 23 March 1949. *Michael H Waller/Online Transport Archive*

One of the systems that had undergone considerable modernisation during the 1930s was Blackpool with a significant number of new single- and double-deck trams — two of which are pictured here — following the appointment of Walter Luff as manager in 1933. *Harry Luff/Online Transport Archive*

damage inevitably and trams were destroyed in Sheffield and elsewhere. Plymouth, with its naval dockyard, was particularly hard hit, although its surviving tramcars managed to continue operating through the heavily damaged streets.

Once peace was restored in 1945, many of the operators that had had conversion plans during the 1930s quickly dusted them off. However, in an era of post-war reconstruction, it was to be some years before many of these systems closed as new vehicles were in short supply and priorities lay elsewhere. There were, moreover, a number of systems that seemed destined for a secure future; with the benefit of hindsight we can see that the hopes were largely thwarted but there were still grounds for optimism in the 1940s with new trams built and new extensions completed.

This, then, is the story of trams in the British Isles in the years immediately following the end of World War 2; it is a tale where the number of operational tramways in the country was in almost inexorable decline and where even the once great systems of places like Liverpool and Glasgow, widely considered in 1945 to be amongst the most secure, ultimately were abandoned.

Another system to be heavily influenced by a pro-tram manager was Sunderland where Charles Albert Hopkins was in charge for two decades. During the 1930s a number of new and second-hand trams were acquired, such as No 28, which was one of three built by the Corporation in 1935. *Harry Luff/Online Transport Archive*

*Opposite top:* Places like Blackpool and Sunderland were atypical, however, and many operators continued to rely on elderly and life-expired trams, such as Blackburn No 47 seen here, which dated originally to 1900. *F N T Lloyd-Jones/Online Transport Archive*

*Opposite bottom:* Another system that operated open-top trams through to the late 1940s was Southampton; No 77 was one of six trams acquired second-hand from the London County Council in 1918/19 that dated originally to 1903. *J Joyce Collection/Online Transport Archive*

# The First Abandonments

Although there were a number of conversions or abandonments during the war, one of the consequences of the conflict was a number of operators actually extended their networks where the infrastructure so permitted. One of these wartime extensions was the Undercliffe route in Bradford, which had been converted to bus operation in 1935 but which was to see trams restored in September 1939 as a wartime measure.

However, one of the consequences of the wartime conditions was that maintenance of both routes and vehicles suffered and there were a number of routes that, as a consequence of this lack of maintenance, were converted with the official sanction of the Ministry of War Transport. Again looking at Bradford, the short section of route from Stanningley to Thornbury was converted in 1942 but sanction for the conversion of the Wibsey route was refused.

By early 1945 it was evident that the war in Europe was moving inexorably towards an Allied victory and, with the return of peace, the future of public transport was back on the agenda. Nationally, the incoming Labour government had a policy of Nationalisation, with the British Transport Commission established to take over the railways, the Tilling Group bus operations, the London Passenger Transport Board and other businesses. Also to be Nationalised was the electricity supply industry; whilst this may not have been perceived as a threat to trams and trolleybuses, the Nationalisation of many municipally-owned power stations, such as Bradford's Valley Road, was to weaken the attraction of electric traction as there was now no perceived benefit to the support of a locally-owned electricity supplier.

The war in Europe was over by the date of the first system to close in 1945. Hull had entered the war with a network of three routes; two, however, had been abandoned in 1942 with 32 of the surplus trams being sold to Leeds for further use, leaving a single route — that running

At the start of World War 2, there were three remaining tram routes in Hull, including route A along Anlaby Road. Despite wartime conditions, two of the three surviving routes were converted, with route A succumbing in September 1942. No 126 was one of 32 trams sold to Leeds for further use following these withdrawals. Hull was to become the first system to close in 1945, with services on the last route being withdrawn in June 1945.
*Barry Cross Collection/Online Transport Archive*

A system reduced to a single route by the outbreak of war was Plymouth and, as home to a naval dockyard, the city was subject to major assault by the Luftwaffe. One raid in 1941 resulted in the destruction of a tram and the suspension temporarily of the surviving route. By 1945, only a handful of trams, including No 165 illustrated here, were operational and the last services operated in September 1945. *F N T Lloyd-Jones/Online Transport Archive*

Although the bulk of the South Shields' fleet was traditional, the operator did possess one modern streamlined car, No 52 as illustrated here, that was acquired from Brush in 1936. When the last surviving route in South Shields was abandoned in 1946, the tram was sold to Sunderland, where, as No 48, it had a further eight years' service. *Brush*

9

Oldham No 123 was one of a batch of 12 cars delivered in 1925 and 1926 that were the last new trams delivered to the operator. Three of the batch, but not No 123, were sold for further service in Gateshead. *Burrows Bros/Online Transport Archive*

from city centre to Dairycoates to survive into 1945 operated by a fleet of less than 20 four-wheel trams, the newest of which dated originally from 1915. The last Hull route was abandoned in June 1945 and, following closure, a further 10 trams were sold to Leeds. One of the ex-Hull cars sold to Leeds, No 132, was eventually preserved as was a 1901-built tram that had been converted to a snowplough in 1933.

Hull, like many of Britain's port cities, had been an obvious target for the Luftwaffe during World War 2; the next system to close had been severely attacked as well. The naval dockyard at Devonport made Plymouth an inevitable target and much of the town was damaged during the war. Prior to the outbreak of war, the Plymouth system had been reduced to a single 3ft 6in-gauge route running from the Theatre to Peverell via Mutley and plans were in place for its conversion before hostilities intervened. Enemy action during the war had resulted in services being suspended briefly following a raid in March 1941 and the destruction of one tram and the damage of another. When services were restored, the route was curtailed to operate from Old Town Street. Although the Plymouth fleet notionally numbered 12 open-top trams, in reality only four were available for service and the last Plymouth trams operated in September 1945.

At the start of the war, there were four tramway systems in the north-east of England. The first of these to close, South Shields, was the first casualty of 1946. Until

One of the smallest undertakings to survive the war was Darwen, which latterly had a serviceable fleet of some five cars including two modern, centre-entrance streamliners built by English Electric in 1936. On closure, both were regauged to 3ft 6in and sold to the Llandudno & Colwyn Bay Electric Railway, where they saw limited service until 1954. *F N T Lloyd-Jones/Online Transport Archive*

the mid-1930s, South Shields had been modernising its tramways but powers were obtained to operate trolleybuses in 1935 with the first being introduced in 1936. Following this, the decision was made to convert the entire system and, by the start of World War 2, only one route — from Moon Street to The Ridgeway — was operational. Between January and December 1943 a second service, the route along Ocean Road, was restored temporarily before being replaced by trolleybuses. Peace saw the surviving one route operated by a fleet of 12 trams, of which five were second-hand acquisitions (from Dumbarton and Wigan) and one was the modern streamline car, No 52, acquired in 1936. The last tram in South Shields operated in April 1946.

The next two casualties were both in Lancashire. The town of Oldham had once had an extensive standard gauge network that included a through service to Manchester via Hollingwood. The process of tramway abandonment had commenced in 1928 and, by September 1939, only two routes survived and both of these had been scheduled to close that month. War intervened and the two routes soldiered on, although that to Shaws Wren Nest was converted to bus operation in December 1939 as a result of the poor condition of the track. The final route, from Hollingwood to Waterhead, operated by some 25 trams, survived until final closure in August 1946.

Bolton No 308 originally dated to 1899 but had been fitted with a replacement English Electric body in 1926. It is pictured at the terminus of the Walkden route, which was converted to bus operation — with the exception of football specials to Burnden Park and a Sunday service to Moses Gate — on 12 November 1944. *Online Transport Archive*

The systems of Manchester and Salford were inextricably linked, although it was the latter that was to abandon its network first. No 350 was one of a batch of 20 trams built as open-top cars by BEC in 1903 and fitted with top covers before World War 1. *Maurice O'Connor*

At the end of World War 2, SHMD operated a handful of serviceable trams, including No 42, which dated originally from 1905, and the board's final public services operated on 12 May 1945 although the official last car, No 18, operated on 29 May that year. However, SHMD track was used by trams from Stockport and Manchester until 1947. *Barry Cross Collection/Online Transport Archive*

Whilst there was a standard gauge network in south Lancashire, in the north-east of county, in and around Blackburn, the 4ft 0in gauge was preferred. Located south of Blackburn, Darwen possessed a small, three-route, system, the major part of which was represented by the joint service between the town and its northern neighbour. Two of the three routes had been converted to bus operation prior to the war, although one of these — to Whitehall — was temporarily restored between September 1939 and March 1940. Although attempts were made to close the Darwen section of the through route during the war, these were rejected and the through service, largely operated by Blackburn as Darwen's fleet gradually contracted to no more than five cars by 1945, survived until October 1946 when the section south of the boundary with Blackburn was converted to bus operation.

The three casualties of 1947 were all in south Lancashire. The first was Bolton, where four services had survived into 1945. More than half of the town's standard-gauge network had been converted to bus operation during the war and, whilst the conflict was to offer a reprieve for the rest of the network, maintenance was minimal and the parlous condition of the track forced the closure — in November 1944 — of the routes to Farnworth and Walkden (although the section of the latter serving Burnden Park survived for football specials until September 1946). With peace restored, conversions resumed in August 1945 with the last route — that serving Tonge Moor — being abandoned in March 1947.

Dominated by the city of Manchester to its east, many Salford Corporation services terminated in Manchester. As with its larger neighbour, the process of converting Salford's trams had started in the early 1930s and, had initial plans for abandonment proceeded, the final trams would have operated in 1940. However, as elsewhere, the war brought a reprieve and three main routes operated by some 60 trams survived. In June 1942 the system grew slightly with the reopening of the line to Weaste, previously a short working on the route to Eccles, although in 1944 the service between Deansgate and Irlam O'th'Heights was suspended as a result of a sewer collapse (it was never restored although peak hour trams continued to operate as far as Pendleton until the route was officially abandoned in November 1945). By the end of the war the operational fleet comprised some 38 cars, although more than 20 others still survived but were unserviceable. One route closed in 1946 — the peak hours service between Pendleton and Trafford Park — leaving the remaining services to close in early 1947. The last Salford tram operated at the end of March 1947.

The Stalybridge, Hyde, Mossley & Dukinfield Tramways & Electricity Board had, probably, the longest name of any British electric tramway. Its once extensive network, which had served the district, had largely disappeared during the period from 1928 through to the mid-1930s but two sections of line — from Hyde to Denton and from Hyde to Vernon Park — saw Manchester and Stockport have running

Bury No 8 was one of a batch of 14 cars constructed by G F Milnes and originally delivered in 1903. Originally built as open-top cars, the 14 were rebuilt as fully enclosed in 1925 and 1926 when they were also fitted with replacement bogies. *S G Jackman/F K Farrell Collection/Online Transport Archive*

powers respectively. Whilst Manchester was progressing with the conversion of some routes to trolleybus operation — and would have converted the route to Hyde sooner had not war intervened and Stockport retained its trams. Thus the SHMD operation survived through the war, although efforts were made — rejected by the Ministry of War Transport in 1944 — to convert the tramways to bus operation as a result of the state of the track. In May 1945 the Board again petitioned the Ministry, this time to withdraw its remaining six trams. This time permission was granted and the final public services operated on 12 May 1945. The final run, however, took place on 29 May 1945 when the last tram was recorded by the BBC. Stockport trams ceased to use the section of line in Hyde in March 1947 and Manchester's final services from Broomstair Bridge to Hyde operated in December of the same year.

No tramways succumbed during 1948 in Britain but 1949 was to see six systems disappear, including the first of the post-war big cities — Manchester — to succumb (see page 28). Also in Lancashire, the three-route system at Bury was to be converted to bus operation in February 1949. The bulk of the town's standard-gauge system had been abandoned during the 1930s, leaving two routes — to Tottington and Walmersley — operational on the outbreak of war. However, as much of the system had only recently been converted to bus operation it proved possible to reintroduce the service to Starkies, close to Bury's football ground at Gigg Lane, as a wartime measure on

Blackburn No 58 was one of a batch of 40 bogie cars built by G F Milnes; originally open-top, all but eight were rebuilt as fully enclosed by 1935. *F N T Lloyd-Jones/Online Transport Archive*

Leicester No 156, seen here picking up passengers with a service for East Park Road, was one of a batch of 10 trams supplied by Brush, built in neighbouring Loughborough, delivered in 1914. Originally built with open platforms, the type was rebuilt as fully enclosed between 1924 and 1934. *F N T Lloyd-Jones/Online Transport Archive*

30 September 1939. To operate these services Bury had some 23 trams, although four of these were sold in 1943 to Bolton. Of the 19 remaining trams, 17 were bogie cars used on the two main routes whilst the remaining two were four-wheel and used on the service to Starkies. In 1945, the service to Starkies was reduced to Saturdays only and was abandoned in July 1946; it was also announced that year that the remaining two routes would be converted to bus operation. The first to close, that to Tottington, succumbed in February 1948 whilst that to Walmersley followed 12 months later.

The next casualty was the last of the Lancashire operators that had adopted the 4ft 0in gauge — Blackburn. As elsewhere, the process of conversion in the town had started in the 1930s; the fact that the fleet — despite the rebuilding of many of the trams between 1920 and 1935 — was increasingly aged and the decline in the local textile industry were factors in the conversion process, which commenced with two routes in early 1939. At the outbreak of war, Blackburn possessed four routes — including the through service to Darwen — and a fleet of 48 trams. With peace restored, the corporation announced that tramway conversion would resume. The first route to be converted — Preston New Road — succumbed in January 1946 although football specials

Rotherham's sole surviving tram route was the through service to Sheffield, for which 11 single-ended trams were purchased from English Electric in 1934 and 1935. No 7 is seen in the company of a Sheffield tram shortly before the service was withdrawn. Following the suspension of the through service, Rotherham's trams were reduced to shuttling to and from a reversing triangle at Tenpleborough. *Unknown Photographer/ Online Transport Archive*

ran later. The next route to close, Wilpshire, followed in December 1947. Two routes survived into 1949. The line to Church was cut back to Intack in January and that south to the Darwen boundary followed six months later. The final section, from the town centre to Intack and the depot, was replaced in September.

November 1949 was to witness the closure of the last tramway in the East Midlands when the standard-gauge system in Leicester was converted to bus operation. The network had been largely intact until the late 1930s, but a report in 1938 advocated its replacement by either bus or trolleybus. Three sections of route succumbed before the war and abandonment would have been swiftly concluded had hostilities not commenced. May 1945, with peace in Europe imminent, the first stage in the city's post-war tramway abandonment saw the Welford Road route converted to bus operation. Between January 1947 and November 1948 a further four sections were converted but the pace of conversion accelerated in 1949 when no fewer than eight routes were abandoned: Groby Road in January; Clarendon Park and Blackbird Road in March; East Park Road in May; Melton Road in July; and, Stoneygate and Belgrave in October. The final route to close was that to Humberstone. At closure, no Leicester trams were preserved, but the body of No 76 was subsequently rescued and restored at Crich.

Across the Pennines, the standard-gauge system in Rotherham had been largely converted to trolleybus operation by 1934 but one route, to Templeborough, survived as part of a through route to Sheffield. As early as 1930 Rotherham had proposed conversion but this had been rejected by Sheffield and, as a result, the former had upgraded its section and bought 11 single-ended trams from English Electric. These, plus one earlier tram (No 12, which was rebuilt as a fully enclosed car in 1942), operated throughout the war with a further tram — No 14 — being acquired second-hand from Leeds in 1942. After the war, the through service continued and Rotherham authorised expenditure on track renewal. However, as a result of bridge work at Tinsley, the through service was suspended in December 1948. Early the following year, it was decided that the new bridge would not carry the trams and that the through tram service would cease. Having lost their primary purpose, there was little future for Rotherham's trams and the service was converted to bus operation in November 1949.

17

Also to be finally abandoned in November 1949 was the last tramway serving the south coast — Southampton. The standard-gauge system had been largely intact until mid-1930s when, in 1935, the service to Millbrook was converted to bus operation; this was followed the following year by the route to Northam Bridge. In 1939, however, workmen's services were restored to Millbrook. As a major port, Southampton suffered considerable attention from the Luftwaffe during the war but the damage to the tram fleet was minimised by the construction of storage sidings outside the town centre. Post-war route closures effectively began in 1948 when the delivery of replacement buses began to be received in significant numbers. By closure in December 1949, the last route to remain in operation was that from Shirley to Floating Bridge, although the line to Portswood remained operational for car movements. One Southampton tram, No 45, was rescued as a result of an appeal following an enthusiast tour in 1948; this was the first tram to be preserved in Britain. Subsequently, a number of tram bodies have been salvaged and are undergoing restoration.

There was only tramway operator in the Manchester area that had entered World War 2 without a confirmed programme of tramway abandonment — Stockport. Although one short section of route — from Cheadle to Gatley — had been converted to bus operation in 1931, the bulk of the system was intact. During the war a certain amount of trackwork was undertaken, with, for example, the section of line along Wellington Road being relaid in 1944 by German prisoners of war. However, whilst Stockport continued to invest in track, further north Manchester had restated its abandonment policy and Stockport was forced to contemplate conversion 'because Manchester will not have anything else'. It was not, however, until July 1949, following the final conversion of the Manchester system, that Stockport's council voted formally to convert its surviving routes and to acquire 68 new buses for the purpose. The first sections to be converted were those to Levenshulme, previously on one of the through routes to Manchester, and Hazel Grove, which were converted in January 1950. Two routes followed in March 1951 — Vernon Park to Edgeley and Mersey Square to Cheadle — leaving one route, Mersey Square to Reddish, again once part of a through route to Manchester, to soldier on to final closure in August 1951.

*Opposite top:* Typical of the Southampton fleet of the period is No 25. The rounded roof was the result of the trams running through the low arch at the Bargate. No 25 was one of the city's last new 'Pullman' trams, which were built by the Corporation during 1930/1. It was among 37 cars purchased by Leeds, of which only 11 entered service including No 25. As Leeds No 299 it was withdrawn in 1953. *W E Crawforth/Online Transport Archive*

*Bottom:* Stockport No 75, seen here at Vernon Park on 15 January 1950, was one of a batch of 10 trams built by Cravens in 1923. These represented the penultimate batch of new trams acquired by the operator and were followed by eight more two years later. Until 1947 it was possible to travel beyond this point on the through service to Hyde. *John H Meredith*

# Grounds for Optimism

Whilst many of the tramways that had survived the war had quickly reverted to a policy of abandonment — now generally in favour of the diesel bus as opposed to the trolleybus — there were, however, a number of operators that sought both to modernise and expand their tramway operations during the immediate post-war years. It was possible, therefore, for the campaigners for tramway modernisation in the Light Railway Transport League to highlight annually extensions and the purchase of new and second-hand vehicles.

It was in Scotland where much of the optimism was engendered. Four Scottish systems had survived the war and none had any plans for conversion. The smallest of the quartet was Dundee, which maintained a compact five-route network operated by 60 trams. Although the fleet was to be reduced by four following withdrawals in 1947, the remaining trams were well maintained and there was also significant investment in new track, with the reconstruction in Albert Square during 1948 and the relaying of the important Murraygate section during 1950. Whilst tentative plans for extensions came to nought, Dundee was generally regarded by enthusiasts of the period as one of the most secure of British tramways.

Three of Dundee's small fleet of four-wheel trams are pictured at Locheé with No 28 on 20 October 1956, the last of the 10 'Lochee' cars delivered in 1930, nearest the camera. These 10 were wider than the rest of the fleet and so were generally restricted to operation of the Lochee route. *Michael H Waller/Online Transport Archive*

In 1939 and 1940, Aberdeen acquired four brand-new streamline trams from English Electric; two, Nos 138 and 139, were fitted with EMB bogies whilst the remaining two, Nos 140 and 141, were both supplied with EMB four-wheel trucks.
*Michael H Waller/Online Transport Archive*

Edinburgh was one of four operators to acquire 'Pilcher' cars following their withdrawal in Manchester. Edinburgh acquired 11 of the types, Nos 401-11, which all entered service in Scotland between 1947 and 1949. The last was withdrawn in 1954. No 407 is seen on Waterloo Place on 25 June 1949.
*Michael H Waller/Online Transport Archive*

Further north was Aberdeen; in 1945 the council agreed on the retention and modernisation of the city's network with the exception of the route to Mannofield, which was ultimately to be converted to bus operation in March 1951 as a result of delays in the receipt of new buses. In furtherance of this policy, 20 brand-new streamlined trams, Nos 19-38, were acquired from R Y Pickering; these were the first trams to be manufactured by this company and, despite contemporary reports seeing the company as a potential major supplier, the reality was that no further orders were secured. Aberdeen's fleet was further strengthened in 1949 by the acquisition of 14 of the 'Pilcher' cars that were then being withdrawn by Manchester. Dating originally to the early 1930s, the other 24 were acquired by Edinburgh, Leeds and Sunderland.

Edinburgh was a relatively recent recruit to electric tramcar operation. The first electric route — other than services outside the city that were acquired when the city's boundaries were extended to include Leith — was opened in 1910 but the bulk of the system was cable-operated until conversion during the 1920s following the corporation's take-over in 1919. The system continued to expand during the 1930s and one route — that to Crewe Toll — saw construction suspended in 1939 as a result of the war; although there were plans post-war to complete the work, this was never undertaken and the part completed infrastructure was dismantled between 1950 and 1953. Although there were to be no post-war extensions, the corporation continued with its policy of fleet modernisation. The last of the converted cable cars was withdrawn in 1947 whilst 11 of the withdrawn 'Pilcher' cars from Manchester were acquired and new trams continued to be built in the corporation's Shrubhill Works until 1950.

The largest batch of new trams delivered to any operator in Britain during the post-war years was represented by the 100 'Coronation II' or 'Cunarder' cars delivered to Glasgow between 1948 and 1952. Unfortunately, almost 30 of the class was to be destroyed in the disastrous deport fire at Dalmarnock in March 1961. Two of type, including No 1297 seen here at Millerston on 23 March 1949, were to be preserved. *Michael H Waller/Online Transport Archive*

The largest tramway operator in the British Isles after the war was Glasgow, with, at its peak in 1948, no fewer than 1,200 trams in service. The Glasgow network was constructed to the unusual gauge of 4ft 7¾in in order to facilitate the operation of conventional railway wagons along the riverside tracks in Clydeside. Although approval was given in 1946 for the introduction of trolleybuses — with the first services being introduced in 1949 (the only new trolleybus system to open post-war in Britain) — this was not seen as the precursor of tramway abandonment; indeed, authorisation was given in 1946 for the construction of 100 new double-deck trams, which were built between 1948 and 1952. Following a fire at Newlands Depot in April 1948, a number of trams were destroyed; these were replaced by eight new or reconstructed trams in 1954 and 1955; these had new bodies but second-hand equipment from Liverpool. The late 1940s witnessed a handful of minor closures, most notably the Duntocher route, but there was also two post-war extensions: Carnwadric (1948) and Blairdardie (1949).

The last wholly new trams to be acquired by Sunderland were four streamlined cars, No 49-52, that were constructed in the corporation's own workshops between 1938 and 1940 on English Electric trucks. No 51 is pictured at the Seaburn terminus of the route via Roker; this service had been suspended during the war and replaced by buses. It was reintroduced on 4 June 1945. *Harry Luff/Online Transport Archive.*

Another system to see a significant post-war extension was Sunderland, where the General Manager, Charles Albert Hopkins, was a noted exponent of tramway development. Appointed in 1929, he had overseen the expansion of the system with the opening of the Seaburn, via Dykelands Road, route from Fulwell in May 1937. To operate the network, Hopkins acquired both new trams, most notably four streamlined cars acquired in 1938-1940, and also a significant number of second-hand vehicles rendered surplus elsewhere. These included eight trams from Huddersfield, Nos 29-36, bought in 1938 and No 100, which was the prototype but non-standard 'Feltham' car from the LPTB. After the war, Hopkins continued to develop the fleet, acquiring six of the Manchester cars, Nos 37-42, as well as South Shields' only streamlined tram when that system closed in 1946. Part of the

The single largest batch of new trams acquired post-war by Blackpool were the 25 'Coronation' cars, Nos 304-28, that were delivered in 1952 and 1953. Manufactured by Roberts, the trams were fitted with the VAMBAC control system that rendered them non-standard with the bulk of the fleet. Two of the type, Nos 323 and 325, are seen passing in front of Blackpool's famous tower. *Harry Luff/Online Transport Archive*

Arguably the most modern first-generation tram to enter service in Britain, Leeds' No 602 was one of three single-deck trams delivered in 1953 and 1954 that were designed for possible use on a planned tram subway in the city. In reality, these plans were never fulfilled and the trio eked out their existence until withdrawal. Nos 601 and 602 were the only trams built by the Leeds-based Charles H Roe and the latter was delivered in a special livery to mark the coronation of HM Queen Elizabeth II. No 602, seen here at Roundhay, was preserved following withdrawal.
*R W A Jones/Online Transport Archive*

rationale for the expansion of the fleet was the Durham Road extension, which was opened in two stages in February 1948 and February 1949. By that date, however, Hopkins had died in office, to be replaced by his assistant, H W Snowball.

The oldest electric street tramway in England was to be found at Blackpool on the Lancashire coast. The system, originally provided with power via a central conduit, first opened in 1885 but had expanded to provide the long coastal route from Fleetwood in the north to Starr Gate in the south (where a connection to the adjacent Lytham St Annes' system existed until April 1937). As with Sunderland, the appointment of a new general manager — in Blackpool's case Walter Luff in 1933 — was critical. At a time when tramways were generally in retreat, Luff argued both for the modernisation of the fleet and the retention of the bulk of the town system alongside the all-important coastal route. Although two routes — Layton and Central Drive — were converted to bus operation in 1936, much more important was Luff's decision to acquire more than 100 new double- and single-deck trams from Brush and English Electric. This meant that the bulk of the fleet was no older than 12 years come peace in 1945; between then and 1954, when he retired, Luff continued his policy of fleet modernisation. One batch of pre-war cars, Nos 10-21, was converted to operate using the all-electric VAMBAC control equipment and allocated to the Marton route whilst 25 new trams, produced by Charles H Roberts and again fitted with VAMBAC control equipment, were delivered during 1952 and 1953. Of all Britain's tramways, Blackpool could perhaps have been regarded as the most secure.

East of the Pennies, two of Yorkshire's surviving systems were also regarded as beacons of potential progress. Leeds entered the post-war era with a significant standard-gauge network and a policy of continued investment in trams. Although the network had been reduced during the 1930s, some of these closures had been offset by the opening of new routes, such as those to Halton in 1936 and to Lawnswood in 1938. In 1940, a further extension, from Belle Isle to Balm Road opened and the track on Compton Road route was doubled in 1942. In 1944, the influential general manager, W Vane Morland, produced two reports to the transport committee on the future of the tramway network. Whilst he recognised that some of the street sections might have to be abandoned, he advocated the construction of a subway network serving the city centre and, in November 1944, these plans were made public. In the immediate aftermath of World War 2 and the need for repair rather than massive investment, these plans were put on hold but the construction of three single-deck trams — two wholly new and one rebuilt from a second-hand tram acquired from Sunderland — showed that the plans were still active.

Whilst little progress was made with the subway plans initially, four short sections of route were converted to bus operation in the late 1940s; again, however, these closures were countered by the construction and opening, in two stages during 1949, of the loop serving Middleton. In addition, the fleet, which numbered more than 450 in 1945, underwent some fleet replacement; although only one new double-deck was built, No 276 in 1948, Leeds acquired significant number of double-deck trams, including eight of the 'Pilcher' cars from Manchester, 37 from Southampton (of which 11 entered service), 90 'Felthams' from the London Transport Executive and the experimental London tram, No 1, which became Leeds No 301 and which was sent in replacement for two 'Felthams' destroyed by fire in London prior to transfer to Leeds.

The second West Riding system to enjoy some investment in the post-war era was Sheffield; as a major centre of the British iron and steel industry, Sheffield had been a major target for the Luftwaffe and a number of trams had been destroyed. This led to the construction of 14 replacement trams between 1941 and 1944 and the purchase of second-hand cars. The war had had another consequence as well; during the 1930s Sheffield had built a number of extensions and had plans to extend further. However, the onset of war meant these plans were deferred and were never to be resurrected. In 1946 the transport department constructed a new four-wheel tram in its own workshops; No 501 was to be the pattern for a batch of 35 new trams built by Charles H Roberts and delivered between 1950 and 1952. These were destined to be last traditional four-wheel double-deck trams built in Britain as well as the last new trams supplied to Sheffield.

In looking at these systems, the proponents of tramway development were, at the time, confident that, whilst may systems were falling by the wayside, places like Glasgow would survive and offer hope for the survival of the tram as a significant provider of public transport in Britain. The next decade was to prove critical.

Apart from the 'Coronation' cars at Blackpool, the Wakefield-based Charles H Roberts also supplied 35 double-deck four-wheel trams to Sheffield between 1950 and 1952. Based around a prototype built by the corporation in 1946, Nos 502-36 represented the last traditional four-wheel trams delivered to any British operator. Two Nos 510 and 513, were preserved following withdrawal in 1960. *Unknown Photographer/ Online Transport Archive*

# The Big Cities Fall

In the immediate post-war years, the first systems to disappear tended to be the relatively small operators — such as Darwen and Plymouth — that had survived because of the war. By the end of the 1940s, many of the bigger cities had also returned to their pre-war policy of tram abandonment or had adopted such a policy in the immediate post-war years.

Of these the first to succumb was Manchester. The policy of tramway abandonment in the city had been developed following the appointment of R Stuart Pilcher as general manager in 1928. Although 38 new fully enclosed trams were built between 1930 and 1932— the 'Pilcher' cars that were to see service in Aberdeen, Edinburgh, Leeds and Sunderland after withdrawal in Manchester — the first tramway abandonments had already taken place and the process accelerated during the 1930s, initially by motorbus and, after powers to operate trolleybuses had been obtained (despite opposition from Pilcher), trolleybuses after 1935. If all had according to plan, Manchester's final tram would have operated in 1942 but the war meant the inevitable revision to the plans. Although one route — Miller Street to Oxford Road — was converted to bus operation in 1940, elsewhere tram services were extended and frequencies improved. The last two service restorations occurred in late 1942 as a result of a request by the Ministry of War Transport to reduce bus mileage by 10%.

By 1945, Manchester still, therefore, possessed a sizeable network, with joint routes operating with Oldham, SHMD and Stockport but, in January 1946, the council confirmed its pre-war plans to convert the remaining tram routes with the diesel bus now the preferred replacement. The first of the post-war conversions followed the next month when services were withdrawn from

Pictured towards the end of the system's life, Manchester No 993, one of a batch of 60 trams built by English Electric in 1924/25, is seen at the Exchange terminus of route 35 to Hazel Grove. Visible in the background is the roof of Exchange station showing evidence of wartime damage.
*F N T Lloyd-Jones/Online Transport Archive*

After the war, the bulk of the Cardiff fleet consisted of some 80 Brush-built four wheelers delivered between 1923 and 1925. These low-height cars were specially designed to pass under low railway bridges. *R W A Jones/Online Transport Archive*

The last tram to operate in Cardiff was No 11, which ran, in a suitably decorated state, on 20 February 1950, the day after the last trams operated in public service. *R W A Jones/Online Transport Archive*

An interesting line up of transport sees, in the background, a Newcastle trolleybus in its yellow livery, and open-top tram No 104 in the foreground. This was one of a batch of Class F bogie single-deck trams built originally in 1901 that had been rebuilt as double-deckers and were amongst the largest capacity tramcars in Britain. Sister car No 102 was secured for preservation on withdrawal. *F N T Lloyd-Jones/Online Transport Archive*

the Exchange to Reddish service via Clowes Street. Over the next three years there was a steady decline in the Manchester network with the result that, by late 1948, only one service, that from Exchange to Hazel Grove, was operational and that was converted to bus operation in January 1949.

The last Welsh municipal tramway operator was Cardiff. The Cardiff tramways had benefited through to 1928 by the management of R L Horsfield, who left to take over at Leeds in 1928. He was an exponent of tramway development under whose auspices there had been a number of extensions and significant investment in fleet modernisation. His successor, William Forbes from Aberdeen, was regarded as more pro-bus and in the mid-1930s, following his recommendation, the first routes were converted to bus operation. In 1939, the corporation decided to introduce trolleybuses and powers were obtained; despite the war, the first section of the new trolleybus network — replacing the trams to Clarence Road — opened in 1942. In 1945 the Cardiff system was operated by almost 90 trams — the newest dating from the mid-1920s — along with 10 trolleybuses in addition to the bus fleet. The avowed policy was still to convert tram services to trolleybus operation but delays in the delivery of new trolleybuses meant that the first post-war conversion — from Hayes Road to Pier Head — was to bus in April 1946. Four routes were converted in 1948 with the penultimate route — from Roath Park to St Mary Street — being converted in December 1949. The final route, St Mary Street to Whitchurch Road, was abandoned in February 1950. None of Cardiff's passenger cars survived into preservation but a water car — No 131 — was saved.

As Newcastle operated joint services with the Gateshead & District Tramways Co, a significant number of single-deckers were required as a result of several low bridges in Gateshead. Typical of these was No 43, which was from a batch of cars supplied by Hurst Nelson in 1901, some of which were eventually completely upgraded in the 1930s. Following withdrawal in 1948, No 43 was acquired for further service by the Gateshead & District.
*F N T Lloyd-Jones/Online Transport Archive*

Bradford No 195 was one of a number of virtually identical open-balcony double-deck trams built in Thornbury Works between 1921 and 1930. Bradford, as a result of its gauge and hilly terrain, was not permitted to operate fully enclosed trams.
*Barry Cross Collection/Online Transport Archive*

Gateshead No 46, seen in Pine Street, was one of a batch of five single-deck trams supplied by G F Milnes & Co in 1902. Originally the five had open platforms but enclosed vestibules were fitted in the early 1930s.
*R W A Jones/Online Transport Archive*

The second casualty of 1950 was Newcastle upon Tyne, where the corporation's system was to be converted in March 1950, although trams continued to operate across the Tyne from Gateshead until the following year. Much of the network north of the Tyne had been converted to trolleybus or bus operation but the planned conversion of the Elswick route in September 1939 was to be delayed; it was converted to trolleybus operation finally in June 1944 using second-hand trolleybuses acquired from Bradford. At the start of the war a number of surplus Newcastle trams were sold for use elsewhere and Sheffield acquired 14 in 1941 to replace temporarily trams destroyed by the Luftwaffe.

By 1945 the Newcastle system had shrunk to a network, apart from the long Throckley route (converted in June 1946), concentrated to the north and east of the city; there were also two links across the Tyne to the Gateshead system on the south. Although tram services were restored to the Gosforth Light Railway for the first time since 1939 in July 1946, by that date the corporation had obtained powers to convert the remainder of the system and had ordered a number of new trolleybuses to start the process. During the next few years, additional trolleybuses were ordered as the final tramways were slowly converted to trolleybus or bus operation: Gosforth in April 1948; Forest Hall, West Moor, Chillingham Road and Shieldhall in October 1948; and, finally, Scotswood Bridge in September 1949. This was the last true Newcastle route as the remaining lines — Saltwell Park and Wrekenton on which Newcastle's trams ceased to operate in March 1950 — were destinations south of the river. This was not, however, to be the end of tramway operation into the city as Gateshead's trams continued to serve Central station until August 1951. After closure, one of the large open-top double-deck trams, No 102, was secured for preservation.

The next system to close was the last of the country's 4ft 0in gauge electric tramways — Bradford. Bradford had been one of the pioneers of trolleybus operation in Britain, with the first services being introduced in June 1911. From the late 1920s the corporation had adopted a policy of replacing trams with, usually, trolleybuses and the network had shrunk considerably by the outbreak of war in 1939 with only some 115 trams in service following the conversion of the Crossflatts route that year. However, with the onset of war, trams were restored to the Undercliffe route in September 1939 and services were extended from Odsal to Horsfall Playing Fields. In 1942, however, the condition of the track forced the closure of the short section from Stanningley to Thornbury although permission to convert the Wibsey route on the same grounds was rejected by the Ministry of War Transport. In the spring of 1944, the general manager, C R Tattam produced a report advocating replacement and, following approval, the route to Wyke and Bailiff Bridge were converted to bus operation in June 1944. Following further sanction, the routes to Wibsey and Little Horton were converted in January 1945. These closures meant that Bradford now had a network of six routes operated by some 100 trams.

Whilst trolleybuses had been the preferred form of transport before the wartime and post-war closures were generally in favour of buses. The first to succumb was the short route to Bowling Old Lane, which closed in December 1947. This was followed by the route to Undercliffe in July 1948; whilst equipment and vehicles to convert this route to trolleybus operation were acquired, it was converted to bus operation. The Bradford Moor route was converted to trolleybus operation in July 1949 and, in December 1949, the long route to Queensbury via Horton Bank Top was converted to bus operation. The penultimate closure, in March 1950, saw the Thornbury service converted with the last route, to Horsfall Playing Fields, being abandoned in May 1950. The last tram, No 104, was sold for use at Odsal stadium; it was rescued for preservation and, fully restored, operated for a number of years along track in front of Thornbury Works. No 104 was the first of many trams throughout Britain to be rescued and restored for preservation.

Although Newcastle Corporation trams had ceased operation in March 1950, the city was to see trams for a further year courtesy of Gateshead & District. This company was one of the subsidiaries of British Electric Traction (BET), one of the country's leading transport companies, to operate trams. Gateshead & District had obtained powers to operate trolleybuses in 1938 but, despite pressure from north of the river, had not invoked them; indeed, after World War 2 the company had both improved the track and had acquired a number of second-hand trams to replace older cars. However, the decision by Newcastle to continue its conversion policy meant that Gateshead was inevitably to follow; powers were obtained to convert in the Gateshead & District Tramways Act of 1950 and the process was concluded rapidly. The last jointly operated tram routes in the UK, to Wrekenton and Heworth, were converted to buses in March 1950 although a few peak hour cars worked to the latter for several months. In March 1951 the services to Saltwell Park and Bensham were converted, followed by Low Fell in April. Teams was converted in July 1951 with the last route, to Dunston, surviving until the following month. On closure, 19 single-deck trams were sold to Grimsby & Immingham; two of these were preserved as was 1901-built single-deck car No 52.

The next city to lose its trams was London. At its creation in 1933, the London Passenger Transport Board had the largest tramway in the British Isles, but the process of conversion to trolleybus operation had already commenced courtesy of London United Tramways. Powers to extend the trolleybus network were obtained in 1934 and 1935; between then and the outbreak of war, the tramway network shrank considerably, particularly north of the river with the surviving trams routes concentrated south of the Thames. There were, however, still more than 1,200 trams in service. The process of conversion continued into the early months of the war, with routes in Ilford being replaced by trolleybuses in November 1939, for example, and those in Barking, East Ham and West Ham in June 1940. With the onset of the Blitz, however, the priority was to maintain some form of public transport and so the process of conversion was halted. The tramways, like much else in London, suffered severe damaged; no fewer than 29 trams, for example, were destroyed in Camberwell depot following a raid in November 1940.

By the end of the war, the London network was some 100 route miles operated by some 870 trams; of the system, 90% was conduit and 10% overhead with the change pits strategically placed where required. Despite the pre-war and wartime conversions, the system was still the second largest in Britain and, in the immediate post-war years, the priority was repair not replacement although conversion was still the plan — but by bus rather than trolleybus following an announcement in November 1946. On 1 January 1948 the London Passenger Transport Board was Nationalised; the final years of tramway operation would be under the auspices of the London Transport Executive.

Although there had been some minor adjustments to the fleet during the late 1940s, including the transfer of the first of the 'Feltham' cars to be sold to Leeds, the watershed came in July 1950 when the chairman of the LTE, Lord Latham , announced a £10 million programme for the final withdrawal of London's trams in a programme codenamed Operation Tramaway. Initially, the plan envisaged conversion in nine stages over a three-year period; in fact, the process was accelerated and completed in eight stages over two years. The first phase took place at the end of

THE BIG CITIES FALL

Again seen on the 38 route, No 1363 was one of the 'E/1' class of tram; this class was built for the London County Council between 1907 and 1922 and represented the single most numerous class of tramcar built in the British Isles. *W E Robertson/Online Transport Archive*

September 1950; this stage also saw the conversion of one of the trolleybus routes to bus operation — an omen for the future of the trolleybus network. The following year was to witness four stages although, in connection with the Festival of Britain, the trackwork in the Waterloo area was upgraded — the last major conduit work undertaken on the network. The sixth stage occurred in January 1952, to be followed by the seventh in April 1952. This stage involved the conversion of the Kingsway Subway routes — effectively the last services to operate north of the Embankment — and thus the closure of the only tramway subway built in Britain. The last stage, scheduled for 5/6 July 1952, was marked by trams operating with commemorative slogans over the preceding week and the issue of special tickets. Following closure, a number of London trams were preserved, with three more being saved later following their withdrawal in Leeds (although one of these was later scrapped following vandalism on the Middleton Railway).

The next casualty was the country's largest operator of 3ft 6in-gauge trams; although standard gauge was generally used on most of the more significant systems, in the West Midlands the narrow gauge was widely adopted and Birmingham had a substantial system using this gauge. Although Birmingham had seen the first tram to trolleybus conversion in Britain — the Nechells route in 1922 — the 1920s had been a decade of considerable investment in the tramways with new routes and trams built. However, in 1930, the Bolton Road and Bearwood routes were converted to bus operation and, in 1934, the Coventry Road route was converted to trolleybus operation. Between 1934 and 1939 the bulk of the network to the east of the city was converted to bus but, as elsewhere, war resulted in the conversion process being delayed although one short section, from Aston to Witton did close (in 1941). In addition 22 trams were destroyed as

London was the only city in Britain to possess a tramway subway; originally built for single-deck trams and opened in 1906, the Kingsway subway was enlarged in 1929 and reopened in 1931 to take double-deck trams. Here one of London Transport's 'E/3' trams heads northbound. The conduit rail used for the central London routes is clearly evident. The final trams used the subway in April 1952. *Geoffrey Ashwell/Online Transport Archive*

a result of enemy action. In 1945, the tramway network was still extensive with some 500 trams available for service.

With peace in 1945 the opportunity was taken to withdraw a number of elderly trams and, in 1946, permission was granted for a number of services to be converted to bus operation. The first post-war conversions took place in March and August 1947 and saw the end of the routes to Lodge Road and Ladywood. The Stetchford routes followed in October 1948 and those to Moseley and beyond in October 1949. Four routes succumbed in 1950: those to Witton and Perry Barr in January and those to Saltley and Lozells in October. The important routes along the Bristol and Pershore roads succumbed in July 1952 (ironically on the same day as the last trams operated in London), leaving three routes — Short Heath, Pype Hayes and Erdington — to operate — until final closure in July 1953. One tram was secured for preservation after closure.

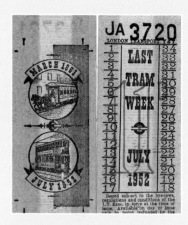

To mark the closure of the capital's tramway system, London Transport issued a set of commemorative tickets in July 1952. The reverse showed one of the original horse trams from 1861 as well as one of the final electric trams of 1952. *Author's Collection*

The last of these major operators to close was perhaps the saddest. Prior to the war Liverpool, under the inspired pro-tram management of Walter G Marks, had one of the most conspicuous investors in a modern tramway network. New vehicles, most notably the 163 bogie streamliners and the cheaper four-wheel versions known as 'Baby Grands' built at Edge Lane works between 1936 and 1942, plus a number of lengthy new extensions on segregated 'grass tracks', meant that the city had one of the most advanced tramways in the country at the start of the war. In early 1948, the Council approved a tramway conversion programme with the result that Marks felt obliged to resign as President of the LRTL. Although miles of track were relaid after the war and scores of war-weary cars rehabilitated, no attempt was made to acquire second-hand cars when 66 trams were destroyed in the Green Lane depot fire of November 1947; as a result, many services operated with reduced frequencies.

The first conversions occurred in June 1948 with a further route following that December. Over the next few years the network shrank considerably. By 1952, when nine routes were converted, almost 30 services had been abandoned. Three were to be converted in 1953 and two in 1954; by this stage, Liverpool had a surplus of modern trams and was able to sell a number of 'Streamliners' (or 'Green

Goddesses' as they were nicknamed) to Glasgow for further service. In addition, a further seven cars were destroyed as a result of a depot fire at Walton in March 1954. By now, the Liverpool fleet had shrunk to some 200 cars and the conversion programme entered its final three years.

Four routes were converted to bus operation in 1955 and further two in 1956. This left two services operational: the 6A from Pier Head to Bowring Park and the 40 from Castle Street to Pagemoss Avenue via Brownlow Hill and Edge Lane Drive. The remaining services were now operated solely by four-wheel trams as the last of the bogie cars had been withdrawn following the conversions in November 1956. The final closure came in September 1957 when the last two routes were converted; the official last tram, 'Baby Grand' No 293, was painted in a special livery for the occasion and was one of two of the type to be preserved following closure. One 'Green Goddess' was also ultimately to be preserved; No 869 was secured following withdrawal in Glasgow.

Opposite top: Liverpool No 765 was one of a batch of 12 cars built in the corporation's own workshops in 1931/32. It is seen here at the Pier Head prior to heading towards Pagemoss on route 40. The 40 was destined to be one Liverpool's last tram routes when converted to bus operation in September 1957. The lower deck of sister car No 762 was preserved in 1977 and has been fully restored as part of the Merseyside Tramway Preservation Society fleet. *John B McCann/Online Transport Archive*

*Bottom:* Two of Liverpool's 'Green Goddess' bogie cars, Nos 909 and 889, pass in March 1954. A number of the type, but not these two, were sold for further use in Glasgow; one of those sold, No 869, was subsequently secured for preservation. *John B McCann/Online Transport Archive*

*Left:* Pictured at Fort Dunlop on 23 May 1950, Birmingham No 609 was one of a batch of 50 cars built by Brush in 1920/21. Birmingham possessed Britain's largest 3ft 6in gauge network. *R W A Jones/Online Transport Archive*

# Across the Irish Sea

In 1945 there were no fewer than six tramways serving Ireland. Two of these — the Giant's Causeway and the Bessbrook & Newry — were amongst the earliest electric tramways constructed in the British Isles whilst a third — that serving a Great Northern Railway (Ireland) branch was one of the last horse tramways to survive in Europe.

At its peak the tramways of Dublin extended over some 60 route miles and had a fleet of some 300 cars; built to the Irish standard gauge of 5ft 3in, the network was controlled by Dublin United Tramways Ltd until 1 January 1945 when, along with the railway network and the majority of bus services, the operator was nationalised as part of the new Córas Iompair Éireann (CIE). Prior to the war DUT had had a policy of converting tram services to bus operation and this process was continued during the war. In late 1944, Ireland suffered a shortage of electricity, with the result that the electric trams serving Dublin and Hill of Howth were suspended. Services on three out of the four surviving DUT routes were restored on 2 October 1944. At Nationalisation, therefore, three routes and some 100 trams survived. The new owners continued the policy of tramcar conversion, with the result that Dublin's last trams operated in 3 July 1949.

The Bessbrook & Newry's depot with Car No 2 nearest the camera. This tram had entered service in *circa* 1935 having been rebuilt from a Dublin & Lucan trailer car. The original body of No 2 had been scrapped and the replacement used the old car's bogies and motors that dated from 1885. This tram was preserved when the system closed. *Real Photographs*

Now bearing the CIE logo on its side, Dublin No 266 was one of 60 'Luxury' trams built in DUT's workshops between 1931 and 1936 on Maley & Taunton trucks. It was in 1938, two years after the last of these trams entered service, that DUT announced that it intended to replace trams over a four-year period. *G Hunter*

Giant's Causeway No 9, originally dating from 1909 but substantially rebuilt in 1945, is seen hauling two well-loaded trailer cars. No 9 was one of three trams from the line to be preserved after closure. *F N T Lloyd-Jones/Online Transport Archive*

Belfast No 297, seen here on the service to Malone Road that was converted to bus operation in November 1951, was one of a batch of 50 delivered in 1921 that had been originally built by Brush. Known as the Moffett class, the 50 were withdrawn between 1951 and 1953. *Martin Jenkins collection/Online Transport Archive*

The Bessbrook & Newry dated back originally to October 1885. Built to the 3ft 0in gauge, the line ran for some three miles and was predominantly powered by a third rail although there were a number of sections at road crossings where overhead was used. The line had been modernised in the 1920s but, by the 1940s, was under threat both from lack of maintenance during the war years and also from the introduction of a new frequent bus service operated by the Northern Ireland Road Transport Board. Although a new timetable for the tramway was introduced in October 1947, that saw only eight return workings per day, this was not sufficient to save the tramway, which closed without ceremony in January 1948. One of the line's trams, No 2, was subsequently preserved and is now displayed in Belfast.

The second of the pioneering Irish lines, the 3ft 0in gauge Giant's Causeway, ran along the Antrim coast, connecting Portrush with the Giant's Causeway via Bushmills. Originally powered by a third rail, an accident in the mid-1890s resulted in the line being converted to operate using overhead power. With the outbreak of war, the line's traffic initially declined, but the establishment of a number of military bases along the coast resulted in a considerable growth in traffic during the war, but this was rapidly to decline again once peace returned in 1945. Operation of the line continued until September 1949 when services were suspended; however, as a result of the company's deteriorating financial position and the unwillingness of the newly created Ulster

The most modern trams operational in Belfast were the 50 McCreary cars, Nos 392-441, that were delivered in 1936. Twenty were supplied with English Electric bodies and the remainder with locally built bodies from Service Motor Works. One of the former, No 427, is pictured on service 57 at Ardoyne in October 1953 just before its withdrawal. All of the city's surviving tram routes were renumbered between 50 and 69 in 1951.
*W E Robertson/Online Transport Archive*

Transport Authority to take over the line, the company's board announced in November 1949 that services had ceased permanently. Although there were efforts to preserve the line, its fate was sealed in early 1951 when the company's assets were sold off in auction. Three of the line's trams have been preserved.

The second city system to survive in Ireland after the war was that serving Belfast. Unusually for Ireland, the Belfast system was constructed to the more usual 4ft 8½in gauge. The system's origins dated back to a horse tramway opened in 1872 with the last electric tramway extension opening in 1925. It was not until the mid-1930s that the first routes were abandoned but, in 1936, the decision was made to convert one route to trolleybus operation. The Falls Road route was converted in March 1938 and, in January 1939, it was decided that the tramway system should be abandoned over a four-year period. With the outbreak of war, such a policy was suspended although a handful of routes were converted to bus or trolleybus operation during the war. In 1945, Belfast still possessed a significant tramway network, with routes serving the north, west and south of the city predominantly. The process of conversion recommenced in early 1945 with the suspension of the Ormeau Road route as a result of a sewer replacement; the tram service was never restored. From May 1946

The Fintona horse tram, No 381, pictured at Fintona Junction in 1957 just before the line closed. The horse, always called Dick (irrespective of gender), was by this date a mare and a single journey over the 0.75-mile route took 10min to Fintona and 15 in the reverse direction. *Unknown Photographer/Online Transport Archive*

onwards the conversion programme gathered pace with the final all-day services operating in October 1953; peak hour services continued through to February 1954 when the official closure was marked.

The last tramway to serve Northern Ireland was the horse tramway that served the short line from Fintona Junction to Fintona, just to the south of Omagh. Originally Fintona had been the terminus of the line, but the opening of an extension to Dromore Road in 1854 resulted in the ¾-mile section from Fintona Junction to Fintona being relegated to the status of a branch. The 5ft 3in-gauge line passed to the Great Northern Railway (Ireland) in 1876 and a new horse-drawn double-deck tram was delivered in 1881. This was to survive through to closure in September 1957 and was preserved on withdrawal. The fate of the line was sealed as a result of the Belfast-based Minister of Commerce's decision to close 115 miles of ex-GNR(I) line in Northern Ireland despite opposition from the south. The closure proposals were confirmed in June 1957 and services were withdrawn three month later.

The last historic tramway in Ireland was another section of the erstwhile GNR(I). This was the line that run from Sutton to Howth stations, north of Dublin, around the rocky promontory known as the Hill of Howth. Serving a popular tourist destination, the 5ft 3in gauge line opened in two sections during 1901. The tramway and its associated railway line passed to the Great Northern Railway Board in 1953 and, in

March 1954, notices of closure for the tramway were issued. However, such was the outcry and the poor state of the local road network that the tramway was reprieved. The Irish government agreed to subsidise the line for at least two years whilst the roads were improved; although the line was doomed once buses were successfully tested in 1957, it was not until May 1959 that the final trams on the line — indeed the final trams in Ireland until the opening of the modern LUAS system in Dublin — operated. After closure five of the 10 passenger trams were preserved, although subsequently one was scrapped in 1965. The bogies from a sixth car were used in the restoration of Manchester No 765.

The last tramway in Ireland was the ex-GNR(I) Hill of Howth, located to the north of Dublin. The line possessed 10 passenger cars that all dated to the first decade of the 20th century. Following closure, a number of the trams were preserved although No 6 was not to survive; its bogies, however, were rescued and, following regauging to standard gauge, were used in the restoration of Manchester No 765. *Paul de Beer/Online Transport Archive*

# The Final Casualties

By the mid-1950s those systems that had had significant pre-war conversion plans and which had survived through to the late 1940s as a result of the war had succumbed. It was now to be the turn of those systems that had seemed to have a secure future in the post-war environment gradually to succumb. Between late 1954 and September 1962, when the once mighty system at Glasgow finally closed, all of the significant urban networks in Britain succumbed.

The first of these supposedly secure systems to close was Sunderland. Despite the investment that had gone into the network in the late 1940s, following the death of Hopkins in 1949 and of his successor Snowball three years later, a new general manager, Norman Morton, was appointed whose agenda was undoubtedly conversion. Whilst two sections of line — the Villette Road route and that to Southwick (the latter as a result of the high cost of tramway restoration following the replacement of a railway bridge) — had been converted to bus operation by the end of 1951, it was announced in September 1952 that the entire system was to be converted to bus operation over a two year period. The process started almost immediately with the conversion of the Grangetown route in November 1952 but the remaining network remained intact until January 1954 when two routes — Circle and Seaburn via Roker — were converted. This was followed by the Durham Road — in part less than five years old — in March 1954 and the last route, Seaburn via Fulwell, was to be converted in October 1954. Following closure, the prototype 'Feltham', by now Sunderland No 100, was secured for preservation.

The smallest of the once secure systems was Dundee but, despite its size, trams held on tenaciously in the city. The last new trams had been delivered in 1930 and the remainder of the fleet had been rebuilt from older trams. As a result, the

When Dundee No 1 was specially decorated for the Coronation in 1953, trams seemed to have a secure future in the city. Unfortunately, the age of the trams — No 1, albeit rebuilt, dated, for example, from 1900 — and the difficulty in obtaining replacements meant that conversion became the preferred policy. *Michael H Waller/Online Transport Archive*

With two Corporation buses in green keeping it company, Sunderland tram No 98 picks up passengers outside the corporation's transport offices in March 1954. No 98 was one of 12 fully-enclosed trams delivered in 1933. Sunderland was unusual amongst British operators in using pantographs.
*Jim Copland*

Two Edinburgh trams, with No 37 nearest to the camera, are seen at Granton in 1951. No 37 was one of 84 trams built in Shrubhill Works post-war and replaced a converted cable car when the latter was withdrawn. Sister car No 35 was preserved after closure.
*R W A Jones/Online Transport Archive*

Aberdeen No 99, dating originally to 1923 when it was built in the corporation's own workshops was originally fitted with a Brill 21E four-wheel truck when new. This was replaced by a Peckham P35. The tram is seen at the Bridge of Don terminus in January 1949; the route from Bridge of Don to Bridge of Dee was destined to be the last tram route in the city. *Michael H Waller/Online Transport Archive*

perceived average age of the fleet was high and the operator was potentially in the market to acquire second-hand trams in replacement. The problem for Dundee was that, apart from the Lochee route where the separation between the two running lines was normal, the narrow streets meant that the gap between the two lines was narrow. Whilst a conventional tram could operate safely on the lines, they could not pass and so the bulk of the Dundee fleet was narrower than usual. Whilst the tracks could have possibly been relaid to accommodate wider trams, the cost would have been prohibitive and there were no narrower trams available from the operators withdrawing more modern equipment and the cost of new trams was prohibitive.

In 1952, Col McCreary, the general manager of Belfast, was asked to act as a consultant; given that Belfast's policy was abandonment, it came as no surprise that he recommended the same for Dundee. At the time, however, the Dundee manager, Robert Taylor, was pro-tram but he was to retire in 1953 and be replaced by W L Russell. One short section of duplicate route — Moncur Crescent — saw services, except football specials, withdrawn in April 1953 but, in late 1954, Russell proposed that the entire system be converted. Despite strong opposition it was decided, in January 1955, to suspend for a trial period the Blackness-Downfield service; this policy was effected in November 1955 when 25 trams were withdrawn and scrapped. In July 1956 the council confirmed the permanent withdrawal of the service and, in order to accelerate the final closure, 25 second-hand buses were acquired from London Transport. Trams

One of the 20 post-war streamlined trams built by R Y Pickering, No 35, heads towards the city centre. Although less than 10 years old when withdrawn, all 20 trams were scrapped following the system's abandonment in May 1958. *John B McCann/Online Transport Archive*

were withdrawn from the final routes — Maryfield-Ninewells and Lochee — in October 1956. Although two trams were made available for preservation, the offer was declined and all of the city's fleet was scrapped.

The following month, November 1956, saw the final operation of Edinburgh's trams. Although the last new tram had emerged from Shrubhill Works in August 1950, the decision had been made earlier in the year for the partial conversion of the system to bus operation. The new policy was confirmed in September 1951 and the first conversion to bus came with the abandonment of the route from Waverley to Comely Bank in June 1952. The following month policy changed again; it was now to be the complete conversion of the system and the revised plan was confirmed in September, despite much local opposition. A second route was converted later the same year, to be followed by two more in 1953. No fewer than eight routes were converted in 1954 and four the following year. This left the city with nine operational routes at the start of 1956. Two of these survivors were converted in March, a further two in May and one in June. Two more followed in September, leaving the remaining two services — Granton Road station to Morningside and Stanley Road to Braids — to operate through to final closure in November 1956. Following closure, one of the post-war cars, No 35, was preserved.

Further north, Aberdeen had undertaken considerable investment and, whilst it had decided in 1945 to convert the Mannofield route to bus operation, even after this service was converted in March 1951 the council reaffirmed its policy of tramway retention. However, this policy was to change in February 1955 when it was announced that the new policy was to be one of total conversion. One route — the Rosemount Circle — had succumbed already, in March 1954, and the next stage in the abandonment programme saw the Woodside service converted in November 1955. The services to Hazlehead and Woodend were converted in October and November 1956 respectively, whilst the route to Sea Beach was suspended between September and December 1956 as a result of the Suez Crisis; this route was finally to be converted in March 1957. The Aberdeen system now

Between 1930 and 1932, 104 'Horsfields' or 'Showboats' entered service in Leeds. These robust ofur-wheelers, Nos 151-254, were named after the General Manager, R L Horsfield. The first four were built by the Corporation at their Kirkstall Road works and the rest by Brush. *R W A Jones/Online Transport Archive*

comprised the single main route from Bridge of Don to Bridge of Dee, which was to survive until final closure in May 1958. Following closure, efforts were made to secure a number of Aberdeen trams for preservation, but none were to survive following the disposal of No 73 that had originally been secured.

Of all the post-war survivors, Leeds had perhaps the most ambitious plans for the future; indeed even as late as 1950 the new general manager, A B Findlay from Glasgow, was pro-tram but a deterioration in the transport department's finances and the election of a new Conservative council led to a reappraisal. Although a short section — from Half Mile Lane to Stanningley — was converted in January 1953, complete conversion was still not council policy. This was to change in March 1953 when the local Labour Party came out in favour of conversion; when Labour took control of the council in May 1953 and, the following month, the new Transport Committee confirmed the policy of abandonment. Two services — Kirkstall Abbey and Compton Road — were converted in 1954, followed by four in 1955, two in 1956 and two in 1957. This left eight services that operated into 1959; three were converted in March that year, one in April, with the remaining four — Harehills Lane, Cross Gates, Halton and Temple Newsam — surviving until final closure. Following the abandonment of the system, a number of trams were secured for preservation; these included two of the three single-deck cars built in the early 1950s — the third was also preserved initially but subsequently scrapped as a result of vandalism — and one of the 'Horsfield' cars of the early 1930s. Two of the ex-LT 'Felthams' were also preserved, although again one was to be subsequently scrapped, and another survivor was the ex-LCC prototype car No 301 (LT No 1).

Built in two batches by Brush (Nos 255-63) and English Electric (Nos 264-71), the 17 cars that became known as 'Middleton Bogies' were fitted with Maley & Taunton swing link bogies and were delivered to Leeds between 1933 and 1935. The last of the type were to survive in service until 1957. *Ray Bicknese/Online Transport Archive*

The final tram operator in Yorkshire was Sheffield; like Leeds an extensive system had survived the war and new trams were delivered as late as 1952. Although the through service to Rotherham had been suspended, then formally abandoned, in 1948, there were no plans for formal conversion until April 1951 when, despite widespread public opposition, it became council policy. The process of conversion started in January 1952 with the Fulwood to Malin Bridge via Hunters Bar service. This was followed in March 1954 by the route from Ecclesall to Middlewood. Two routes — Walkley to Elm Tree and Elm Tree to Intake — succumbed in 1956 to be followed by Crookes to Handsworth and Exchange Street to Sheffield Road Top via Newhall Road in 1957. Further closures came in 1958 and 1959, leaving a handful of routes operating into 1960. April 1960 saw the conversion of the Sheffield Lane Top to Woodseats/Meadowhead service with the final route — Beauchief to Weedon Street — succumbing in October 1960. At closure, a number of trams were again secured for preservation, including two of the Roberts cars, Nos 510 and 513, that had received commemorative side panels recording the city's 90-year tramway history for the closure ceremony.

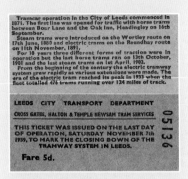

Tramcar operation in the City of Leeds commenced in 1871. The first line was opened for traffic with horse trams between Boar Lane and the Oak Inn, Headingley on 16th September.

Steam trams were introduced on the Wortley route on 17th June, 1880 and electric trams on the Roundhay route on 11th November, 1891.

For 10 years three different forms of traction were in operation but the last horse trams ran on 13th October, 1901 and the last steam trams on 1st April, 1902.

From the beginning of the century the electric tramway system grew rapidly as various extensions were made. The era of the electric tram reached its peak in 1933 when the fleet totalled 476 trams running over 124 miles of track.

**LEEDS CITY TRANSPORT DEPARTMENT**

CROSS GATES, HALTON & TEMPLE NEWSAM TRAM SERVICES

THIS TICKET WAS ISSUED ON THE LAST DAY OF OPERATION, SATURDAY NOVEMBER 7th 1959, TO MARK THE CLOSING DOWN OF THE TRAMWAY SYSTEM IN LEEDS.

**Fare 5d.**

Leeds, like a number of other operators, issued special tickets on the occasion of the last tram. The reverse of the tickets contained a brief history of tramway operation in the city since 1871.
*Author's Collection*

LEEDS CITY TRANSPORT DEPARTMENT

SEAT RESERVATION
ON
**LAST TRAM**
SATURDAY, 7th NOVEMBER, 1959

ISSUED TO
PASSENGERS ARE ASKED TO BE AT SWINEGATE DEPOT (MAIN GATES) AT 6.0 p.m. ADMITTANCE TO THE DEPOT TO BOARD THE LAST TRAM WILL ONLY BE GRANTED ON PRESENTATION OF THIS TICKET.

TRAM NO.

A pass, illustrated here, was required by those travelling on the official last trams in Leeds on 7 November 1959.
*Author's Collection*

The last of the big city systems to close was the largest of them all — Glasgow. Whilst there had been a couple of minor conversions during the early 1950s, by the end of 1953 the city's tram fleet numbered some 1,100 cars of which 258 were modern, alongside 74 trolleybuses and 835 buses. Much investment over the previous three years had gone into the new trolleybus system but Renfrew, one of the areas through which Glasgow's trams operated, had voted to see the tramcar retained and the council had voted funding for alterations to the trackwork in the borough. In 1954, the general Manager, E R L Fitzpayne, produced the first of a series of important reports. In it he recognised that almost half of the fleet was life-expired, of which 100 needed to be replaced urgently. The purchase of ex-Liverpool trams had helped the situation and more were to be acquired. In 1955 he proposed a limited plan for closing 10 routes over a five-year period that would permit the withdrawal of 300 older trams. This policy was approved in April 1955 and was further modified in February 1956 when the corporation decided to close a number of sections — most notably in Paisley and Airdrie — outside the city's boundaries. However, despite these decisions, in late 1956, the council voted against proposals for the complete abandonment of the system.

During these years there had been some minor conversions in furtherance of the planned network reduction but, in June 1957, a report was presented to the Transport Committee that showed that to modernise the existing tram fleet would cost more than double the cost of bus replacement and 50% more than replacing the system with trolleybuses. Given the life expectancy of the more modern trams, it was thought that the system would survive until the early 1970s. In February 1958, the City Council approved the conversion over a period of up to 15 years; however, in August 1958, there was to be a further revision to the policy — the trams were still to be converted but the process was now to be accelerated and be completed within five years.

Two generations of Sheffield tram make their way towards the city centre. Closest to the camera are Nos 109 and 217; these were both built in Sheffield's own workshops during the early 1930s. The third car is one of the Roberts-built four-wheel cars delivered between 1950 and 1952. *Unknown Photographer*

Once the decision to convert the entire system had been made, the closures came rapidly. Three routes had closed earlier in 1958, but five more followed by the end of the year, to be followed by seven in 1959 and six more in 1960. By the start of 1961 the once mighty fleet had been reduced to 300 and only nine of the 'Standard' cars remained in service. These and a number of other elderly trams were to survive longer than anticipated as a result of a serious fire at Dalmarnock Depot on 23 March 1961 when some 50 trams were destroyed; those lost included four of the 1954 replacement 'Coronations' and resulted in the temporary return to traffic of a number of withdrawn cars, including some set aside for preservation. During 1961 a further five routes were withdrawn leaving three routes and almost 190 trams in service.

The first of the three — from Anderston Cross to Baillieston — was converted in March 1962, to be followed by the route from Clydebank to Dalmarnock in July 1962. The last route — the 9 from Dalmuir West to Auchenshuggle — was converted to bus operation in September 1962. As with the closure of the London system a decade earlier, the final obsequies in Glasgow were marked by the production of a documentary film — *9 Dalmuir West* — and the memory of Glasgow trams was to be further ensured through the preservation of a number of the cars following withdrawal.

Sheffield No 71, one of the trams built in the corporation's own workshops, is pictured on the service to Woodseats in Fitzalan Square. *Phil Tatt/Online Transport Archive*

Apart from these systems, there were three other operators that had survived into the second half of the 1950s but which were to close by 1961. The first of these was the Llandudno & Colwyn Bay in North Wales. This was the last 3ft 6in gauge tramway to operate in Britain and dated originally 1907 with extensions opening in 1909 and 1915. Cut back at its western terminus in 1917, in September 1930 the section to Old Colwyn was abandoned, to be replaced by Crosville buses.

The L&CB was company owned, unlike the majority of post-war tramways that were, with the exception of Gateshead, Grimsby & Immingham and Swansea & Mumbles, all owned by local authorities. In the late 1940s the company had invested in acquiring the two ex-Darwen streamlined cars, although these were not a success as Ministry of Transport tests resulted in them being restricted in use, whilst much of the track was also to be repaired. Less positive was the gradual erosion of the coast at Penrhyn Bay that ultimately resulted in the line being singled through this section. In addition, although carrying significant numbers of seasonal passengers, its financial position was deteriorating and losses were incurred. The possibility that the line might be converted to bus operation resulted in proposals for its preservation, although these came to nothing. In September 1955 the company acquired its first bus but difficulties with the

Traffic Commissioners and an unresolved issue of road restoration meant that the trams soldiered on. The death knell, however, was not long in coming; in early 1956 the electricity supplier — MANWEB — announced a significant increase in charges and led L&CB board rapidly to decide to abandon the route. The final trams operated on 25 March 1956. After closure, one of the ex-Bournemouth cars was secured for preservation.

In order to bolster its fleet and replace a number of the increasingly aged 'Standard' cars, Glasgow entered the second-hand market in 1953 and 1954, acquiring no fewer than 46 'Green Goddesses' from Liverpool. No 1020 is seen at Tollcross on 22 May 1954. *Michael H Waller/Online Transport Archive*

The Swansea & Mumbles line in South Wales had its origins in the Oystermouth Railway and was thus the oldest passenger-carrying line in the world. Electrified in 1929 — the last wholly-new first-generation electric tramway in Britain — the line was operated by 13 106-seat double-deck trams supplied by Brush that were amongst the largest ever supplied for use in the country. The tramway was controlled by South Wales Transport, a subsidiary of British Electric Traction. Whilst serving a popular destination for day trippers from Swansea, in the

Trams of two eras pictured at Lambhill on 9 April 1958. Closest to the camera is 'Standard' No 779, which dated originally to 1900, whilst 'Cunarder' No 1333 was built in 1950. Following withdrawal, No 779 was to be preserved by the Corporation as one of a number of trams for display. *Paul de Beer/Online Transport Archive*

years after World War 2, passenger numbers started to decline and, from the mid-1950s, South Wales Transport started to examine the possibility of conversion to bus operation. In order to achieve this, parliamentary powers to abandon the line needed to be obtained; this was achieved through the South Wales Transport Act that was passed, despite objections, on 29 July 1959. The first section of line to close, from Southend to Mumbles Pier, succumbed on 11 October 1959 to permit the construction of a replacement road; the rest of the route from Swansea followed on 5 January 1960. Following closure, one of the 13 trams was preserved; unfortunately, vandalism resulted in its scrapping although the cab section of a second tram does still survive.

The final one of this trio was the last railway-owned tramway in the British Isles — the Grimsby & Immingham. Historically, the railways had owned a number of tramways but only one passenger-carrying tramway survived the war. Built originally by the Great Central Railway to ferry worker to the newly opened docks at Immingham, electric services commenced in 1912. Passing to the LNER in 1923, the line was Nationalised in 1948. In 1951, the tram's livery was altered to green and the fleet was supplemented by the acquisition of 19 surplus trams from Gateshead, of which 17 entered passenger service. These arrivals allowed for the withdrawal of certain older trams. However, the first threat to the tramway came in 1955 when British Railways offered the short street section in Grimsby to the council; this offer was taken up and six second-hand buses were acquired to replace the trams. This meant that the section from Pyewipe to Corporation Bridge was converted to bus operation in June 1956. By the late 1950s, the finances of operating the line were deteriorating and, in the summer of 1958, BR applied to close the line. Permission was, however, refused although revised bus routes introduced in 1959 resulted in the reduction in the number of trams required. A further attempt to close the line was announced in December 1960 and, with the number of objections reduced, permission was this time granted. The Grimsby & Immingham operated for the last time on 1 July 1961. After closure, one of the original GCR trams as well as two of the second-hand Gateshead trams were secured for preservation.

Llandudno & Colwyn Bay No 8 was one of 10 cars acquired second-hand from Bournemouth in 1936. Nine of the cars had originally been built by Brush between 1921 and 1926; the 10th, No 6, dated originally to 1914 and had been supplied by UEC. No 6 was to be preserved on withdrawal. *Jim Copland*

The last company-owned tramway in Britain to operate was the Swansea & Mumbles. The line was the last wholly new electric tramway to open in Britain prior to World War 2, dating from the late 1920s when 13 large Brush-built trams entered service. The trams were unusual in only having doors on one side — the landward — and were also amongst the largest trams ever delivered in Britain, with a seating capacity of 106. The cab from sister car No 7 is preserved in Swansea. *Chris Bennett & Martin Jenkins/ Online Transport Archive*

One of the Grimsby & Immingham's original trams, No 3, heads west towards the dock with a sister car in the distance. One of this type, No 14, was secured for preservation following the line's final closure in July 1961. *Chris Bennett & Martin Jenkins/Online Transport Archive.*

# The Survivors

With the closure of the once impressive system in Glasgow in September 1962, the traditional tramcar in the British Isles was all but extinct. There remained one system in Britain where street running remained — Blackpool — but even here the early 1960s witnessed a considerable decline in route mileage with the abandonment of all of the routes that had survived the war with the exception of the long service from Starr Gate in the south to Fleetwood in the north.

In 1954 Walter Luff retired, to be replaced by Joseph Franklin — another exponent of trams. Although the transport department's finances were not as strong as they had been initially, the late 1950s seemed to hold considerable promise for the future. In 1957, the track from Squires Gate to Starr Gate was uncovered and a unidirectional, seasonal circular service that had operated prior to the war was reintroduced and, in the following year, the complex and important junction at Royal Oak was relaid. In 1958, two 'railcoaches', Nos 276 and 275, were transformed into a motor-car and trailer set to test the principle of tram/trailer operation with the result that 10 unpowered trailers — Nos T1-T10 — were built by Metropolitan Cammell-Weymann and eight further railcoaches were remodelled to haul trailers. No 275 eventually reverted to being a power car.

One of the two 1903-built cars serving the upper section of the Great Orme tramway is pictured at the summit in 1957. *Paul de Beer/Online Transport Archive*

This view of Devonshire shows one of the Luff 'railcoaches' working on the Marton route. This line was also home to the rebuilt pre-war 'Sun Saloons', Nos 10-21, which had been transformed between 1948 and 1952 into comfortable 48-seaters with VAMBAC control. All the Marton 'Vambacs' were withdrawn in October 1962 when this — the last traditional all street track electric tramway in the country — was replaced by buses. *Chris Bennett & Martin Jenkins/Online Transport Archive*

With a Corporation AEC Regent on the right, two horse trams, No 10 from the mid-1880s and No 21 from 1890, pass in front of Villiers Hotel in Douglas during 1956. *John B McCann/Online Transport Archive*

Manx Electric toastrack No 27, the last of a batch of three delivered from G F Milnes & Co in 1898, stands in front of Derby Castle as it heads, with a trailer, towards Douglas during the summer of 1956.
*John B McCann/Online Transport Archive*

However, despite the promise of the late 1950s, in 1960 it was decided that the cost of relaying the Lytham Road route could not be justified and it was announced in October 1960 that the line would be converted to bus operation; it last operated in October 1961. The closure of this route affected the financial position of the Marton route — as it had benefited from the operation of the circular service — and it was announced that the route would close. The last trams operated over the Marton route in October 1962. By now, tramway closures were becoming an annual event in Blackpool and the last section of the street tramway — Dickson Road — was converted to bus operation in October 1963 — the last tramway abandonment in the British Isles. Blackpool's trams, however, survived on the long Fleetwood to Starr Gate route, with a fleet of trams largely dating from the 1930s. Some of the non-standard 'Coronations' had their troublesome VAMBAC equipment replaced by conventional equipment from older cars and, as such, the last examples soldiered on until 1975.

The only other tramway to survive in mainland Britain is not a true tramway but rather a funicular — the Great Orme. Operating in two sections from Llandudno to the Summit, the line opened in two stages in 1902 and 1903. Operated by four cars, two on each section, built by Hurst Nelson, the 4ft 0in-gauge line was taken over by Llandudno Council in January 1949. A popular tourist attraction, the line underwent some modernisation during the 1950s. Whilst fitted with overhead, this was not designed to provide power but rather aid communication between the drivers of the trams.

Three of the surviving tramways in the British Isles are located on the Isle of Man. Of the three, the most anachronistic is perhaps the 3ft 0in-gauge horse tramway serving the promenade in Douglas. First opening in 1876, the tramway had been taken over by the corporation in 1902; although there were plans to electrify the route, these were never completed. Operating during the summer months, services ceased in September 1939; they were not to be resumed until May 1946. In November 1947 the council voted to retain the tramway although the number of trams was to be reduced; following this decision, all bar one of the double-deck trams were withdrawn as were a number of single-deckers. Following these withdrawals, the fleet numbered some 30 trams by 1950 although the number was further reduced by a modest number of withdrawals during the early 1950s. During the decade the trams continued to operate although, as elsewhere, their financial position deteriorated; despite this, however, a further attempt to abandon the route was rejected in the early 1960s.

The Manx Electric Railway provides a link from Douglas northwards along the coast to Ramsey. The first section, from Douglas to Groudle Glen, of the 3ft 0in-gauge route opened in 1893 and it was completed through to Ramsey in 1899. Surviving in private ownership, by the mid-1950s the company's finances had so seriously deteriorated that, towards the end of 1955, the company announced that, without government support, the line would close at the end of the 1956 season. In early 1956 consultants from British Railways advocated to the Manx government that the line be converted to bus operation; this proposal was, however, rejected by the Manx parliament and a stay of execution was agreed whilst the future of the line was determined. In November 1956 it was agreed that the Manx government would take over the line; in June 1957 ownership was transferred to the new Manx Electric Railway Board with a new livery of green and white being adopted in 1958. Although initially there were problems over the size of the annual subsidy, over the next five years much of the line's infrastructure was upgraded ensuring its survival into the 1960s and beyond.

Linked to the Manx Electric Railway, but constructed to the different gauge of 3ft 6in to accommodate the centre third rail necessary for the Fell gear and braking system required to enable the trams to ascend the mountain, the Snaefell Mountain Railway operates from Laxey, where it meets the MER, to the peak of Snaefell. The line opened in 1895 and, like the rest of the MER, passed to the new Manx Electric Railway Board in June 1957. Alongside the line's primary tourist traffic, during the early 1950s the number of passengers was boosted by Air Ministry staff that used it and the MER to gain access to the mountain for the construction of a new radar station. Throughout the period the line was operated by six G F Milnes & Co trams delivered for the line's opening.

Thus the story of the tram in the British Isles during the immediate post-war years draws to a close; from some 50 systems at the start of the period, the number of tramways had declined to six operating less than 200 trams in all. Today those six have been joined by a number of second-generation systems and by a number of highly successful preservation operations; but that, as they say, is another story.

Two of the Snaefell's six trams, Nos 1 and 2, are pictured outside the line's depot at Laxey. Built by G F Milnes & Co in 1895, five of the type remain in service; the sixth was destroyed by fire in 1971 and subsequently rebuilt. *Geoffrey Morant/Online Transport Archive*

# Index